Common Sense 2.0:

America's Identity

By: Ryan F. Murphy

Table of Contents

Introduction

For far too long, the United States has been playing this game of Left vs. Right, Liberal vs. Conservative, Republican vs. Democrat. Since the 1990's both sides have gone farther to their extremes, more so on the Democrat side than on the Republican side. Its time for this to stop and start using Common Sense! It's this very Common Sense that led to the creation of our great nation. In January of 1776, Thomas Paine published a book by that very same name: Common Sense. This book was read aloud in pubs, taverns, and public gatherings all across the 13 colonies. It called for the American Independence from Great Britain. It was only Common Sense that an island, thousands of miles away across an ocean, shouldn't have say and control to a people that would come to inhabit an entire continent.

This book was inspired by that same Common Sense in order to tackle today's issues. We will take an in-depth look at the problems that are plaguing the American people today and offer common sense solutions to those problems. I strongly feel that if you are going to bring light to an issue, you must also present a viable solution; if not you are just complaining. And nobody like complainers, they solve nothing. I hope to keep this as nonpartisan as possible, but some of these views will lean left and right. But the point is to offer Common Sense. It will ask each of you to take a look at yourself and determine if the mindset that you currently have is helping or hurting the country. It will challenge each of you to see things from the point of view of a person who you disagree with. And it will challenge each of you to, as President John F. Kennedy has said, "Ask not what your country can do for you. Ask what you can do for your country".

As you are reading this book, drop your political bias and keep an open mind. It doesn't matter if you are a Republican or a Democrat, set that aside as you are reading this and my hope is that one day everyone will drop their political party affiliation for good. After all, one of the warnings our first President, George Washington, gave during his farewell address was against the creation of political parties. Look where not listening to him got

us.

Chapter 1

The Problem

What if I told you that a fire just broke out and burned

down hundreds of thousands of homes leaving half a million

people homeless. What If I told you that ISIS was launching an

attack on the United States everyday, killing more than 1,600

people a day? What if I told you that major corporations were

ripping off their customers to the tune of $10,000 a year in false

advertising? I think we all would demand action and take to the

streets to protest until something got done.

Well I just changed the villain in those situations. Instead

of a fire burning down homes and leaving half a million people

homeless, there are already half a million homeless people in the

United States, and I believe the number is much higher than that.

Instead of ISIS killing more than 1,600 Americans a day. That

evil villain is cancer. Instead of large corporations ripping people

off and not delivering on their promises, that villain has become colleges and universities. Its time for a change. Its time to see the real problems happening in this country.

So what should happen? Most people would say this is where the government has to step in and start some kind of program, relief effort, or new regulation. That is absolutely not the answer to the problems we face today. It is time that we stop turning to the government to solve our problems, can they help? Absolutely. Can they be the permanent fix? No. Where does this fix come from? You and Me.

The first step to fixing any problem is to identify that there is a problem. We can no longer rely on the media to do their job and report on the real problems facing all of us today. The media is so focused on their ratings and shareholders, that they have lost sight of their true purpose. Problem solving. Now the media only reports on topics that will create controversy. Why? Because we are all drawn to it. I'm just as guilty as you at getting drawn into heated debates about divisive topics, but it's just a distraction. The media even makes up their own controversies to draw in viewers. Because viewers mean ratings, and rating mean they can charge higher prices for their commercial slots, and higher commercial slots means the products they are selling must go up in price. Is there anything wrong with that? I don't believe so. It's the world we live in today.

People go do crazy stunts on YouTube to gain more followers to increase their ad money. People release sex tapes in order to gain fame and launch clothing lines and TV shows. And people go on TV to preach about how God wants them to have another Private Jet so their followers will buy them one.

Not every problem has to have a solution. You just have to learn how to work around, see through, or use the problem to your advantage. That's how you work smarter not harder.

So what can you do? I'm not saying to turn off the news, I'm saying to be aware of how they make money so you can understand why they are reporting on what they are reporting on and try not to get caught up in the small potatoes arguments.

Focus on the bigger picture. Or do one even better. Use the media to your advantage.

The best example of this was Donald Trump. He knew what the media covered and then went out and said/did what they would cover. He completely controlled the news cycle. Tweet in the morning. Have the news outlets like CNN and MSNBC outraged at his tweet. Hold a rally and explain his tweet and then have Hannity come on at night and praise him for speaking up. And then it would all start again the next day.

So either use the media to your advantage or see through it. Now lets get on to figuring out the problems.

Chapter 2

Health

According to WorldLifeExpectancy.com the United States ranks 34th in the world in life expectancy, which happens to be just below Cuba which is 33rd. How could that be? With all of our modern breakthroughs in technology, the new surgeries we've developed, and all of the prescription medications. Cubans live longer than Americans.

How can we change this? Spend more money on prescription drugs? We already spend more money than everyone else in the world, a including the next 10 countries on that list combined. Should we ban Monsanto and GMOs from our food supply? Any new regulation is just gong to make it harder on our farmers. Should we switch to a socialist healthcare system? No Way! Look at the UK and Canada. The quality of healthcare there is garbage and when someone really gets sick, they come to the United States for treatment. Look at the heartbreaking case of the little sweet English baby Charlie

Guard. The government wouldn't allow his parents to take him to a different country. You can't ration medical care.

So what can you do? The answer is to educate yourself about health and care about what goes into your body. Now am I saying that you can't eat McDonald's ever again? Of course not. Their hotcakes with sausage is one of my favorite breakfasts, I don't want to, give that up. It's about moderation and balance. It's also about where your food comes from. Anything processed is not going to be good for you. Any food that has a commercial is also not going to be good for you. The best way to buy your food is to buy locally grown. On average it takes 15 calories of energy in order to transport 1 calorie of food. The food isn't going to be the best quality, It's bad for the environment, and it helps your local farmer to buy from them.

What to look for in your food? Obviously with your fruits and vegetables you are looking for Organic and Non-GMO. Imagine if everyone would stick to organic and Non-GMO. Monsanto would go out of business without one law or regulation being passed. That's how you make real change. Demand and purchase a better product! You can also grow your own food at home! If done properly it can be simple, fun, and rewarding. How do I know this? I have my very own little garden in my backyard. Nothing tastes better than a homegrown, organic, Non-GMO carrot! Imagine becoming good enough to not have to go to the grocery store for your produce? And you don't need too large of an area to do it. Even a small patio can work for certain vegetables.

What about your meat and diary? Tyson is the largest chicken manufacturer in the country. Yes I said manufacturer not chicken grower. In the chicken houses they have 3 to 4 birds in a cage without enough room to even sit down. Usually one of the birds is dead and the others are feeding on it. These chickens never see the light of day and all the manure they produce in that single spot makes the area become toxic because it is so concentrated. It's very sad and disturbing.

Chicken are omnivores and love to eat insects, the only protein they get inside these grow houses are other chickens! (I know, gross) Chickens are natures garbage disposal and should be treated as such by letting them scratch around outside for insects and eating grass in the sun. They are not supposed to be eating corn all the time!

If you look at a farmer by the name of Joel Salatin, he and his team at Polyface Farm let chickens be chickens. All of his meat birds never touch the same ground each day where they are able to eat all the things chickens are supposed to eat. At the same time the chicken manure is being spread out evenly across the pasture and making nutrient rich grasses grow abundantly!

The same can be said for his cattle. Cattle are nature's lawn mowers and should be treated as such! In most cattle farms the cattle are either penned up all day in dirt or spread out over large acreage. Joel's way of doing things is so much better. Joel's cattle are 100% grass fed from start to finish. Cattle in pens are fed corn (which they aren't supposed to eat) and in some cases other cows (again ew gross), which leads to the outbreak of mad cow disease! Joel keeps his cattle in small areas on the pasture, which are called paddocks, held in by electric fences. By replicating what the bison did on the Great Plains by mob grazing, the cattle end up eating most of the grass in that paddock which includes the bad invasive grass. So by using the cows as a lawn mower he is able to keep his cows 100% grass fed, improve his pasture by allowing the better clover type grass to grow, improve the soil by the cows dropping 50 pounds of manure to help the grass grow, and help the environment because the cows eating the grass will force new better quality grass to grow and soak up more carbon dioxide and produce more oxygen. This is the balance that I am taking about.

Joel even takes it a step further, because of the manure flies that are attracted to the area, leaving fly larvae in the manure. Joel then has what he calls the eggmobile that holds his egg laying chickens, follow the cattle and they spread the manure out and eat the fly larvae. Again look at this balance! If you want to find out more about what Joel does you can look him up on YouTube and read his books. The way he raises his pigs will shock you!

Remember, the best way to treat disease is to prevent it. It's been proven that eating non-processed food is much healthier, and on top of it buying local produce and meat grown this way will vastly improve your health.

Now that's what you can do about your food. What about what you drink? It is finally starting to come out about how bad sugary drinks like soda are for your health. Now full disclosure here, I am an independent distributor for a company called Enagic®. They are a medical grade water ionizer company. I am going to promote the products because I believe in them extremely strongly and it's not some sort of shameless plug. Enagic produces a machine that makes Kangen Water™. It is by far in my opinion the healthiest water on the planet. What makes the water so different is its three distinct properties. The water is Alkaline, Anit-oxidant, and microclustered. Without getting too scientific, the three main causes for disease are dehydration, over

acidity in the body, and free radical damaged cells. The

microclustering (or smallness of the water clusters) hydrates you

on a cellular level, which helps with the dehydration, the anti-

oxidant property neutralizes the free radicals, and the opposite of

acid is alkaline. Now Enagic® doesn't allow us to make medical

or health claims because of the FDA standards; but I'll tell you

what, this is what leaving acidic drinks and bottled water did for

my family but just keep it between you and me so I don't get in

"trouble." The water helped get rid of my sister's migraine

headaches, got my mom off of arthritis medication, helped my

aunt with chronic fatigue, and that's just a little bit of what it has

done for my family, not even including how it helps with acid

reflux, gout, and other issues. If anyone at the FDA is reading

this and has an issue with the "claims" I am making here, you

need to rewrite you regulations because they are preventing

people from getting rid of their issues. These are real, tried and true accounts, and if you don't believe me try the water and come talk to me after a month.

Staying away from soda, energy drinks, and sports drinks can really benefit you. Most people don't know that the ph. of soda is so acidic that it takes 32 cups of 9.5 Kangen Water™ to neutralize 1 cup of soda. The amount of acid you are drinking is severely damaging your health.

The number one cause of death for kids 14 and under is cancer. That is completely unacceptable. If you were born prior to 1970 think back to when you were a kid. Were your friends having to go to the nurse during lunchtime to get their diabetes insulin? Did you see kids walking around school with scars on their heads because they were undergoing chemotherapy? No of course not! What changed? The diet of kids starting at 3 years old is a happy meal and a soda. Again this isn't about banning McDonalds or Coca Cola; it's about moderation and balance. Simple changes in diet and what you drink can severely impact the health of you and your family.

Healthcare

Now let's talk about the unfortunate people that are already

sick. The healthcare in this country is a mess. The number one

cause of death in the United States is cardiovascular disease.

Second on the list is cancer. Third, I would have guessed, is

diabetes, but its not. It's complications with prescription drugs.

Shocked? I know, I was too! Remember the best way to avoid

this is to prevent disease from happening at all. Now I don't want

to seem like I'm anti medication, I am medication as a last resort

and much more into preventative medicine.

The problems with the way we go about prescription drugs

is that the government (which really means the American

taxpayer) helps fund the research and development of the new

and upcoming drugs. They should continue to do this and

actually increase the funding. At the same time they should be

cutting the red tape in which drugs that could help people don't

take 17 years to get to the marketplace. But the problem is that

the companies that we invest in for their research and

development then turn around and sells us the drugs at retail price. The American Taxpayer owns part of the drug and should be entitled to a steep discount, not only for owning it but an additional discount for bulk purchases such as Medicare.

This is also an opportunity for the country to make some money. Because we were the ones that funded the drug and own part of it, we should be entitled to a percentage of the profits from the drugs being sold in other countries. This money should then be used to fund our health care system and reduce the burden on Americans.

Now let's speak on the health insurance currently in place in the United States. Right now we really don't have health insurance. We have Sick Insurance. We need to completely flip the system on its head and instead of paying doctors when we are sick; we pay doctors when we are healthy. Radically different? Absolutely! We should treat the health care system like you would a gym membership or any other subscription type service.

The average doctor currently has 2,500 patients. Instead of

paying them when we come into see them, we pay them (for example) $50 per month when we are healthy and we pay them nothing when we are sick. This way we will ensure that the doctor's number one goal is to maintain their patient's health, instead of getting kickbacks from the drug companies for being pill pushers. There will have to be many more nuances added to this to ensure that everyone gets covered. Mainly those people with pre-existing conditions, because they MUST be covered as well. Also with the doctor's sole focus on the patient's health the number of malpractice lawsuits should decrease and we can put provisions in order to make it harder for patients to sue doctors such as a mandatory loser pay legal fees.

If you think about it, it would be a great deal for doctors. 2,500 patients multiplied by $50 per month each. That's a potential $125,000 a month multiplied by 12 months, which comes out to be $1.5 million a year. But with part of that they will have to pay their staff and overhead.

Now is what I am describing to you the be all end all scenario? Of course not, there are many other factors that must go into play, such as specialists, hospitals, therapy, and so on. But it is a starting point and a base of how to run a medical system that promotes doctors getting paid for keeping their patients healthy, while also cutting costs for everyone.

The average family of four spends $14,300 a year on health insurance premiums according to businesswire.com. This translates to $1,191.67 a month. This plan would allow the average family of four to pay $200 per month ($50 x 4), for a potential savings of $991.67 a month or $11,900 a year!

An improved focus on health and a huge cost savings. That's what anyone would call COMMON SENSE! Just remember that the person that is most responsible for your health is you!

Chapter 3

Money and Education

The plan of going to school, getting good grades, going to a good college, and finding a job, IS DEAD! Over the past 20 years we have pushed that a college education is the key to success, all the while ignoring the laws of supply and demand. The more kids go to college; the less and less special a degree really makes them. You see, when colleges first began it was incredibly special for someone to get in to a school, let alone to graduate with a degree. The degree made them stand out when applying for jobs. Today a degree means nothing because everyone has one.

One of the first questions millennials ask each other, is "Where do you (or did you) go to school?" When they come across someone that didn't go to school, they almost seemed shocked. This is because EVERYONE is going to some sort of higher education school. Essentially this has devalued the college degree. (Remember the Law of Supply and Demand).

Let's take a look at a common college major. Lets choose Marketing for example. After graduating from school with a marketing degree, students join the workforce and apply for jobs related to marketing. If you go onto ZipRecruier.com or Indeed.com, you will find that there are fewer marketing positions available than applicants applying for those positions by a wide margin. So again, back to the Law of Supply and Demand! The supply of the job is low but the demand for the job is high, putting the employer in a much better negotiating position in terms of compensation. Why? Because if you have 5 applicants with all the same schooling and skills; which one as the employer would you hire? The one that would require the least amount of money! This leads to the decline in pay for that degree!

Now instead of recognizing that the Laws of Supply and Demand are working against the people with a marketing degree, they get sold this idea that they just need to stand out more in order to get the position. So what do they do? They go back to school to get a Masters in marketing, only further going into debt and starting the trend all over again.

If this continues, Masters Degrees wont be special anymore, just like high school diplomas and Bachelors degrees, and that's a problem! As degrees become more worthless, the price of college keeps rising. This forces people to take out more school loans, which can't even be removed by bankruptcy.

Some people might be thinking that I'm anti-education, and that is simply not the case. I read more books, watch more instructional YouTube videos, and go to more training seminars than 99.9% of the population. I'm all for education, but it's just the type of education that should be different. The solution to the problem is teaching Entrepreneurship and Trades.

Remember this, the easiest job you can get is the one that you create yourself.

I want you all of you have graduated high school to think back and ask yourself the question "What did I learn in high school that I currently use in my life today?" Still thinking? Of course you are, you might be able to count on one hand the number of lessons that you were taught in high school that you are able to use today.

For me, I was able to name 3. How to take a poll in stats class, the quote "you must learn history, if not you are doomed to repeat it", and not to mix ammonia and bleach (it creates nerve gas, don't do that). But that really was it. Mind you that I went to a Private Catholic School for my four years of high school.

Today's curriculum is a joke. High school teachers have now become glorified babysitters. And that is not a slight against the teachers; it's the system they operate in that tells them what they have to teach. That brings me to Common Core.

Common Core was sold as a "No child left behind" curriculum, and in theory it would be a great thing. But it soon turned from elevating the children on the bottom to catch up with the children on the top, to holding the top down to the level of the kids at the bottom. Holding a child back and not allowing them to realize their true potential is one of the greatest sins of humanity.

So what is the solution? To give the power of what is taught in schools back to the community, so that way the people can teach students life skills they can use forever.

The two most important classes that a student can take in high school are Economics and Health. If you know how to be healthy and if you know how to handle money, you can easily thrive in this country and live a long and happy life. So why is it that students are only required to take 1 semester of each? Instead, students are taught 2 years of algebra and another year of learning how to do proofs in geometry. When was the last time that you used algebra in your daily life? And helping your kids with their homework doesn't count! I'm not saying that there is no need for algebra, but it should only be taught in the specific professions that require it. This promotes natural learning, which means "Learning on an as –needed basis." Or another way of saying it is learning by doing. Which is by far the more superior way of learning. Remember this, "Learning occurs when someone wants to learn, not when someone wants to teach."

So back to the point I was making about the subject of Econ and Health. Imagine, instead of learning how to graph a parabola, you learned how to open a business, balance a checkbook, fill out a tax return, or cook a healthy low cost meal. You know, skills that you'd actually use.

The whole education system is teaching people how to be employees, down to the bell schedule. You show up at 8am and the teacher takes attendance (clocking in), then you get a 15-minute break and another 30-minute break for lunch. You have to get permission to go to the bathroom and you are told when you are allowed to go home.

The lower levels of the education system should be about teaching the basics of reading, writing, math, history, and basic science. But once in high school, it should be about finding what a kid is passionate about and helping them realize their true potential within that passion, along with basic needed life skills.

A teacher should be the most proud when a former student comes up to them and says, "because of what you taught me, it helped me open a successful business within my students passion." This takes us into Entrepreneurship.

America represents freedom, but are we truly free when most people are a slave to their work? You see, the only reason to have a job should be so that you don't need to have a job anymore. If you have to work in a factory, in a cubicle, or in a field that you don't own, it should be in order to set yourself up to liberate yourself from your job. The American Dream is based around being your own boss. I am in no way shape or form demeaning anyone for having a job, but given the opportunity the vast majority of people would rather be their own boss than report to one.

Find out what you love to do, create a viable business plan around it, and begin working for yourself and building your own dream, not someone else's. Some people out there might be saying "But I'm not an entrepreneur." The response to that is "Of course you are!" You make entrepreneurial decisions everyday! The home that you invest in, the coupon that you use at the grocery store, and even the type of gas you put in your car. Why? Because each decision affects your very own bottom line, which is your bank account! The American Entrepreneurial Spirit is the greatest thing the world has ever known. It brought us the telephone, the light bulb, the automobile, the Internet, the smartphone, and countless other spectacular innovations! What can you do? What are you good at? What lasting impact can you have on the world? The answer is definitely something amazing! The key is finding out how to unlock it! Never Ever Ever Forget This…. DREAM BIG!

Trade Schools

The art of learning a trade is dying. That being said, there are plenty of high paying trade jobs. Everything from a Welder to an HVAC Tech to a Crane Operator to a Plumber to an Electrician to a Millwright. The problem is, society tends to look down on these professions and say that those are the jobs for the uneducated people. Well the reality is that these "uneducated people" are making more money working with their hands, than the "educated" people are working in a cubicle. Why is that? It comes down to the same answer, The Law of Supply and Demand.

Now is there anything wrong with either of these career routes? Absolutely not. But you have to understand that the more people go to college the less your degree will be worth and the more trade jobs will increase their wages to attract potential workers.

Trade jobs are also more scalable, which means that it is much easier to grow them into a business rather than just a job. This is where that American Entrepreneurial Spirit Comes into play and takes away the notion that with a trade job, you will end up having to work until you die.

Let's use the example of a plumber. A plumber starts his own plumbing business and builds his reputation as a great plumber due to his excellent quality of work. When someone needs a plumber they call him to do the job. As the plumber begins to gain work, he will soon need to either hire an assistant plumber or take on an apprentice. If he hires an assistant, he will most likely end up training his competition and it will end up hurting him in the long run (Law of Supply and Demand.) But if he looks for an apprentice that he invests time with and trains with the option of eventually becoming a business partner with, he creates leverage in his income stream.

The plumber lets the apprentice that he trained; use his company name and reputation to generate more customers, while keeping a percentage of the profit that the apprentice has generated. Why would this benefit both parties? The hardest thing in business is to generate a trusted brand and reputation. By doing this, you can cut marketing and advertising costs way down. The apprentice uses the trusted brand to work under and the plumber uses his trusted brand to make money without working. This is the key to financial success. Leveraged Income!

What is Leveraged Income? It is income that you generate without working. Multi-Billionaire Warren Buffett says "If you don't find a way to make money while you sleep, you will work until you die", and it is very true. This is where the American Education System lacks so heavily. It only teaches people how to get a job. Remember, the only reason that you should work is so you don't have to work anymore. Emphasis on the words HAVE TO because if you love your job, then don't quit. But you want to put yourself in a position to where if you get tired of your job you can stop working at anytime without it affecting your income.

This brings us back to the plumber. He now has 5-10 apprentices working for him but running their own businesses, each paying him 10% of their profits for using his company name. The plumber no longer HAS TO work, because he's making money on other people's efforts. Billionaire Oil Tycoon J.Paul Getty says it best, "I'd rather have 1% of 100 peoples efforts, rather than 100% of my own." This is Leveraged Income!

This is why people invest in Stocks, Bonds, Precious Metals, Real Estate, and open Franchises. It's to make money while you are sleeping. This is the key to freedom. My mentors don't even think about the social security income that they are going to be receiving. Why? They simply don't need it. They have leveraged themselves enough throughout their lives so that they are already financially set.

This is the kind of thinking that needs to be taught in schools. The best selling book "Think and Grow Rich" by Napoleon Hill should have an entire year's worth of classes dedicated to it. The book is based on Napoleon Hill interviewing the 500 most successful people of his time, including Henry Ford, Thomas Edison, Alexander Graham Bell, and Andrew Carnegie. He then takes their combined teaching and experiences, puts it into a book, and allows everyone to learn from it. By the way, you can get it on Amazon for as little as $3.66.

Think about it. Who would you rather have your kids learn from? Mrs. Cooper, who just got her teaching credentials, or the Billionaire Andrew Carnegie? The choice is blatantly obvious. It's this kind of thinking that our education system needs. It's this kind of thinking that will help unlock the potential in each child. It's this kind of thinking that will spur major advancements for the future of mankind. But it's also the kind of thinking that will help people remove the financial stress that most of us face today.

Chapter 4

Taxes and Regulations

It's been said that Death and Taxes are the two things you can't avoid during your life. It's true. The United States was founded on the over-taxation by the British of the 13 original colonies. That's really what Thomas Paine's Common Sense book was about. That's what the phrase "No Taxation without Representation" is really about. Today the phrase of the current tax system should be "No Taxation For Those With Representation" What does that mean? Look at Amazon for example. They have become the richest company in the country and they paid ZERO in federal income tax. How could this be? The answer is the lobbyist.

Avenue K in Washington DC is where the real creatures of the swamp live. Lobbyists for huge corporations are the people that really make the laws in this country. Why? Because they control politicians, whether it be through endorsements, kickbacks, or blackmail.

Lobbyists control politicians to make laws that help their

clients. This is so obvious with the tax laws.

We've all heard the saying; "It's harder to stay King

than to become King." This isn't true for big business

today. Why? Because the tax laws and regulations enacted

make it so difficult for new companies to start up. New

startup companies spend more money on lawyers than on

Research and Development. We need to make this

country's tax laws small business friendly.

You see, in order to start a business today, it takes

capital (money). You can either save up the money

yourself, take out a loan, or fund raise. If you take out a

loan, you put yourself at risk. If you fund raise, you have to

give up a portion of your business. But if you can save up

the money yourself, you keep 100% controlling interest

without having to put up any collateral.

Today's tax environment makes it extremely difficult for average, everyday people to save money. The average American Household pays 22-24% in income taxes which translates into an average of $8,367.00 a year. If you include state income taxes, the number rises to over $10,000.00. This is money that people who receive a W2 won't ever get to see in their bank account, and this is money that people who receive a 1099 will have to pay at the end of the year.

Imagine if there was a tax system that was simple, fair, and allowed people to save money? There is one. Completely eliminate the federal income tax. Some people might say that's too radical. And others will say where will the country get money from? The answer is a federal sales tax of 10%. This way the rich will end up paying more in taxes because they will spend more money, and the poor will pay less in taxes because they will spend less money. It's completely fair for all parties involved. At the same time this allows for people to get ahead and get some breathing room.

Imagine seeing the money that is taken out of your paycheck for taxes, placed into your bank account! What would you do with it? It would be a god send for most people. The only trade off would be that goods would be slightly more expensive, but you wouldn't get punished for making money any longer.

Again, like the health care system, there are variables that will need to be hashed out; but the basis of a 10% federal sales tax and the complete elimination of the federal income tax should be the basis for the tax system. It would level the playing field to close loopholes left open that huge corporations take advantage of.

Some ideas with the 10% federal sales tax would be to not tax items such as fruits and vegetables, and possibly to do a 15-20% tax on alcohol, tobacco, and marijuana products. This would help promote healthy eating by making it more affordable for families to eat healthier.

The focus of this would be a system a tax system that would remove the government from punishing people for making money, allow people to save, and have an equal playing field for people and corporations alike to pay their fair share of taxes.

Chapter 5

Trade

Let's talk about trade in terms of sports. If you have a football team and you have a great Quarterback, 6 great Wide Receivers, and a terrible Running Back, you aren't going to trade for another Quarterback or a Wide Receiver. You will use common sense and trade for a good Running Back. Why? Because you don't need a Quarterback or a Wide Receiver, you need a good Running Back. Now what will you trade for the Running Back? You only have 1 good Quarterback so you wont be trading him. But you have 6 good Wide Receivers, and you only need 3 or 4. So you trade from your surplus of Wide Receivers to get a good Running Back. This is just common sense.

But this isn't what our country does. We ship in millions of cars from overseas from places like Japan, Korea, Germany, and Italy, when we have perfectly good car manufacturers here in the United States. Ford, Dodge,

Chevy, Buick, Chrysler, Jeep, and all of the other US car manufacturers can easily build and sell enough cars to satisfy everyone here. This would also create millions of jobs for Americans. Essentially what we are doing is bringing in more Wide Receivers!

Now am I saying that Mercedes, BMW, Audi, Toyota, Kia, Jaguar, and other foreign cars shouldn't be sold in the United States? No, but they better be made here. There is absolutely no reason why a foreign automobile assembler should be taking the place of an American one. If someone in the United States wants to purchase a car manufactured in a different county, they better be paying an extremely high tariff.

Now with the way the North American Free Trade Agreement (NAFTA) is structured US car manufacturers can move to Mexico and take advantage of the extremely low wages paid to Mexican workers to assemble cars. Then they get driven across the border at Zero tariff and sold to

Americans, all the while taking American jobs. President Trump has been spot on, calling these trade deals and the people that make them STUPID!

Free Trade can be a good thing, as long as it's fair trade. When Mercedes imports a car from Germany, they currently pay a 2.5% tariff, but when Ford imports a car to the European Union, Ford has to pay a whooping 25% tariff! 10 TIMES MORE! That is not a fair trade deal; it's a stupid one for us.

We have a great advantage over many other countries just based on our land mass and Geography. We inhabit what basically amounts to the entire useable part of North America. From the Atlantic to the Pacific. From Canada to the Gulf of Mexico. Even the tropical island paradise of Hawaii to the freezing Tundra's of Alaska. When someone asks what the climate of the United States is, they have to specify what part. It's not like that for most countries. For example, Russia is cold. Egypt is hot.

Vietnam is Humid. Somalia is dry.

Same goes for the question of Topography

Switzerland is in the Alps. India is in the Dessert. Australia

is mostly flat. In the United States we have it all. From the

white sandy beaches of Florida, to the forests of

Washington and Oregon. From the Rocky Mountains of

Colorado to the Great Plains of Kansas to the swamps in

Louisiana to the desserts of Arizona and New Mexico to

the Great Lakes of the rust belt to the rivers flowing

through the Bible Belt. Even take a look a California, you

can start the day surfing of the coast off Huntington Beach,

snowboard at noon on the slopes of Big Bear, dirt bike in

the High Deserts near Barstow and make it back to the sun

setting over the ocean while eating dinner on Catalina

Island, all in the same day.

The point is, there is very little that we need to

import from other countries. We have taken advantage of

the cheap labor in countries like China for many years, but at the cost of losing Billions of Dollars a year in trade deficits. If we use the natural resources we have and learn to replenish them and make them stronger along the way, we can blow every other country away economically and environmentally (which we will discuss in a later chapter)

The argument against imposing tariffs is that it will make goods more expensive. Which is true, and I could get into how it will strengthen the dollar, but Newt Gingrich says it best, "We'd rather people buy American made goods anyways!" We have to remember the world needs us much more than we need them. We don't want to shut ourselves out from the world, but its time that we throw around our economic might and enforce the golden rule. "He who has the gold makes the rules" It's time for us to start calling the shots and start profiting from other countries, like they have been doing off of us for so many years. This is a key for us to start to solve the debt

situation.

Chapter 6

Immigration

Before starting this chapter, I want to make two things perfectly clear. There is a difference between Legal Immigration and Illegal Immigration. And that America is the world's greatest melting pot built as a nation of immigrants. That being said, Immigration should have nothing to do with race and everything to do with need and merit.

Right now there are approximately 320 million Americans living in the United States. We are a distant 3rd to China and India. Regardless, 320 million people is a lot of people. I'm from Los Angeles County, where the infamous 405 freeway runs through. During rush hour traffic it is not uncommon for it to take and hour to go 10 miles.

It makes it difficult for people to be able to get around, especially how spread out places are in Southern California.

When it comes to Immigration, like I said earlier, it should be based on NEED and MERIT. We are going to tackle each of these one at a time. When I say Immigration should be based on NEED, it directly relates to the unemployment numbers and average wage. If there are currently not enough jobs for Americans, why are we going to be bringing in more people that need jobs? That makes absolutely no sense. It's time that we use Common Sense on the immigration issue. We should only bring in workers when we don't have enough people to fill the jobs we currently have open.

Then secondly, we have to look at wages. From 1990- 2016 wages, in terms of real dollars remained stagnant. Why? Let's go back to the Law of Supply and Demand Again. Demand for jobs was high and Supply of

Jobs was low, so this made wages not increase. We have to create an environment that flips this situation, where the supply of jobs is high and the demand for jobs is low. This will force companies to pay higher wages in order to bring on and retain good employees. If we halted immigration, and created a business friendly environment with taxes, we would achieve this. Only then is there a need for immigrants, because we need people to fill the jobs left open, but when wages begin to stagnate we need to stop the immigration again.

This might sound harsh but its reality. If you think about it, we will be creating an extremely strong economy and country for the immigrants to come into and put them in the best situation to succeed.

Now to the second issue, MERIT. We only need to let people in this country who can take care of themselves and benefit our society. This Lottery system and chain migration is a joke. You shouldn't be given an American citizenship; it should be earned, just like everything else in this world. Who would benefit America more: Bob the bum who has no skill and will need government assistance to survive, or Juan the carpenter who already has a job waiting for him? How about Suzy with 4 kids and no working skills need to go on welfare immediately or Kathy who is a grade school teacher and has already completed her United States teaching credentials? This is just Common Sense people. NEED and MERIT are the Common Sense solution to Immigration.

Now for the more controversial topic, Illegal Immigration. Let me ask you a question. Do you lock your front door at night? Of course you do! Why? So people don't come in without your permission. It's the same thing with our borders. WE MUST BUILD A WALL! A country without borders isn't truly a country. We are the only country in the world that freely allows people to pass through our borders unchecked. So before some of you start screaming racism, last time I checked Illegal wasn't a race. Even Mexico has a giant fence on its Southern border with Guatemala.

Upwards of 85% of the heroin coming into the United States comes across from the US- Mexican Border. This is a big problem. Some people might say that the wall won't work. Look at the places where a wall/fence is already in place. Illegal crossings are way down in those areas. We must have a system in place to immediately deport all crossings. As of right now, the catch and release program is still in effect. So even when border patrol agents catch someone, they are scheduled a court date years from now and hardly ever show up. All the while remaining in the United States. How stupid is this policy! We must amend the laws to immediately send people back the way they came.

Now as for the Illegal Immigrants already in the country, we must accept our failure to act. We cannot go around and deport the 11-12 million people already living here. We must make a deal with them. First off, any violent and drug trafficking criminals MUST be deported. NO EXCEPTIONS, we don't need that in our country. Second, the good hard working people that are here must pay a $1,000 per person fine for breaking the law. That money, $1,000 multiplied by 12 million, is $12 Billion will be put towards the building of the wall. Even former Mexican President Vincente Fox has said that a wall between the US and Mexico would be a good thing. Even going so far as saying Mexico will pay for half of it. So with Mexico's half and the money collected from the Illegal Immigrants staying here, that is $24 Billion to pay for the wall. None of which the United States Taxpayer pays.

Now, the people staying are not given citizenship, but are given a green card that comes with a taxpayer ID. This way it resolves the issue of Illegal Immigrants not paying their fair share. This would end up being a huge benefit for these people, being able to come out of the shadows and live the American Dream like they came here to do.

These people would be able to take advantage of the labor laws in place to ensure that they aren't taken advantage of any longer. We can even let them finance the fine they will have to pay. But the only way this works is to enforce a Zero Tolerance Illegal Immigration Policy the day this is implemented.

Chapter 7

Homelessness

This is the problem that no one wants to talk about.
Politicians don't care about homeless people because
homeless people by in large don't vote. It's a problem
affecting every major metropolitan area in the country.
Less than 2 miles from the house I grew up in, there is a
new, very large, homeless camp created in an alley. It was
starting to get so bad that the city brought in port-o-potties
so that people aren't going to the bathroom on the
sidewalk.

It's been said that there are over 600,000 homeless
people in the United States, but after traveling all around
the country I am convinced that the number is much higher.
It's time to help these people put a roof over their heads
and become productive members of society.

Why are these people homeless? For a wide variety
of reasons, drug abuse, mental illness, bad decisions. One

of my mentors Daniel asked me a very intriguing question one day. He said that if you rank people on a financial scale of 1 to 100 with Bill Gates being number 1 and the last homeless person you saw being number 100 how does a homeless person just move to 99? They can't do it on their own. Being homeless, you can't hold a job. On every job application you have to put a valid address. If these people can't even apply for a job how do they get out of the situation they are in? The answer is that they don't unless they have help.

I have no data to back up this claim, but I truly believe that with the right deals made, $5,000 can get people the counseling, rehab, temporary housing, and food in their stomach to be able to get them back up on their feet. Now am I saying that you should go give a homeless person a check for $5,000? NO! How many people have $5,000 laying around to give to a homeless person? Not many. But I do believe that most people have $9.38 to give.

Why do I say that number? Because if each person gave $9.38 we would be able to give each homeless person $5,000 worth of care to help them get back up on their feet.

The answer to defeat homelessness is not in a government program or a super large "charity" that keeps 85% of the money for "administration fees". The answer is in a group of people, focusing on one homeless person at a time to make their life better.

This sounds too simple to work, but sometimes the most simple and genuine things are the things that work the best. I'm not a person who is all talk and no action so I plan to start a gofundme.com page for a homeless person and help them become a productive member of society. I hope that each of you will donate $9.38 to help the person we choose to help. I hope to make this a blueprint that can be replicated all over the country.

Chapter 8

Common Sense

In this Chapter we are going to go over quick points of common sense that most people agree with.

- Money in elections: Only people or entities that have a vote should be able to donate to a candidate's campaign or Super PAC. Corporate money should not be allowed. Why? A corporation can't vote only citizens can. This will help politicians from being controlled by special interests.

- Gay Marriage: The government shouldn't be allowed to control who people marry or go to bed with. To the people against it, I have only one question for you. Does it affect you in any way? No, so let people do what they want to do.

- Genders: There are only 2 genders, stop trying to make up new ones. To the people that say there are more than two, what is the third thing in between people's legs? There is a Penis and a Vagina. Nothing else.

- Transgender Bathroom/Locker Room Laws: Simple solution that has to deal with the last statement. Whatever is between your legs is the bathroom you use. If you have the surgery to change your sex, then again you can use the bathroom of whatever is between your legs. To the people against this: do you really want men in the same locker room changing with a 6 year old girl/

- Pedophilia: It is not a sexual orientation. It's a crime and any offenders should be put to death and/or castrated

- Military Action: We should stay out of everyone else's business, with only the exceptions of an imminent national security threat, containing nuclear expansion, and mass genocide. We are not the world's police and we shouldn't act like it, we only make enemies this way.

- Voter ID: You must be able to show that you are eligible to vote. You need an ID to drive a car and to buy alcohol, tobacco, marijuana, and lottery tickets. You have to show ID in order to gamble. And above all, it's required by law that you have ID on your person at all times. If you can't get an ID and prove you are eligible to vote, then you don't vote.

- Marijuana: Legalize it and impose a heavy sales tax. It's a plant that is non addictive. The only studies that have shown it's addictive are biased government funded studies.

- The Gold Standard: We need to switch back to a currency that is backed by a precious metal, such as gold. Even an overall precious metal standard would greatly increase the strength of the dollar and wouldn't allow the FED to control our currency.

- The Deficit: We are borrowing money from ourselves. That doesn't make any sense. We need to absolutely control our spending, but it doesn't make sense to borrow from ourselves. The FED needs to be disbanded or at the very least audited.

- Abortion: This is not a good thing. The people out there saying they wish they had an abortion just so they can say they had one are troubled people (Lena Dunham). I'm not saying to make it legal or not. That power should be given to the individual States so the people can vote. But abortion should be held to the same standard as if in the extremely tragic event that a pregnant lady got murdered. At what point does the murderer get charged with double murder? Both Women and Baby have rights. At what point does the baby become a baby? That's the question you have to ask yourself. At what point does it become a double murder?

- The Outlawing of Political Parties: This gives too much power to unelected people. George Washington warned us against them. This forces people to choose between the lesser of 2 evils. More competition means better results.

- Guns: The Second Amendment protects the rest of the Amendments. Never give up your guns! At the same time, people on the terrorist watch list shouldn't be allowed to purchase guns or ammo. Gun training classes should be required for first time buyers. All common sense solutions, but never turn in your guns. Guns give the people the power, and the people that are trying to take your guns are trying to take your power. Chicago, which has the most gun laws, also has the most gun related crimes and murders. More gun laws does not translate into safer cities.

- The Electoral College: This must remain in place! Why? Because if it wasn't, presidential candidates would only campaign in New York, Los Angeles, Chicago, and a few other major cities because of their population volume. It forces candidates to take into account the needs of people in places like Fargo, North Dakota, Columbus, Ohio, Tulsa Oklahoma, and Abilene Texas.

These are a few hot button issues that common sense can fix and solve. Again, like with all of the ideas presented in this book, these are just starting points that will need to be built off of and that aren't be all, end all solutions.

Chapter 9

America's Identity

Think back to the last time someone asked you the question "What are you?" What did you say? Did you say German? Italian? Chinese? Mexican? Black? Filipino? British? Or some combination? When was the last time that you said American? Maybe last time you were out of the country? You probably said something like "I'm from the United States, but I'm (insert family country of origin here)"

You see, in this country, there are some many factions trying to divide us. In elementary school everyone played with everyone, it didn't matter the person's skin color. Everyone was friends with everyone. You just thought people's skin was lighter and darker than others. It's not until you have your first standardized test that you have to put on paper what you are. Most of the time, the teacher has to explain what race is to help students fill out the form correctly.

The United States is, as Former President Bill Clinton said, "A nation of immigrants." The definition of immigrant according to Webster's Dictionary is: "a person who comes to live permanently in a foreign country." The problem is that in order to be a successful immigrant you have to embrace the country that you are joining. The best way to put it is to use the saying "When in Rome, Do as the Romans Do." Even back in 2004 at the Democrat National Convention, then Senate Candidate Barrack Obama, in his speech, said "E Pluribus Unum, out of many, one.... Well, I say...tonight, there's not a liberal America and a conservative America; there's the United States of America. There's not a black America and a white America and a Latino America and an Asian America; there's the United States of America."

He goes on the say "the pundits like to slice and dice our country into red states and blue states… But I've got news for them, too. We worship an awesome God in the Blue States, and we don't like federal agents poking around our libraries in the Red States. We coach Little League in the Blue States and, yes we've got some gay friends in the Red States." Then the most important line of his speech: "We are one people, all of us pledging allegiance to the stars and stripes, all of us defending the United States of America."

My question to former President Obama… why didn't you work to do this? He did the opposite and divided the country even more. It's his party that started the trend of Identity Politics. Even Chance the Rapper Tweeted "All blacks don't have to be democrats." Because it's gotten to a point to where you are expected to vote based on your skin color. Candice Owens' YouTube video about coming out as a conservative highlights this.

Oh and by the way Hillary, half of all Trump supporters aren't Deplorable!

It's time that we focus on E Pluribus Unum (it's the motto of the United States), out of many, one. It's time to stop calling ourselves African-Americans, Latino-Americans, White- Americans, Asian-Americans, Native Americans, etc. It's time for us to just all be Americans! I'm not saying that you need to leave behind your cultures or traditions, I'm not. I'm Half Mexican and Half Irish. I'm not going to stop eating tamales on Christmas Eve, celebrating Cinco de Mayo, or St. Patrick's Day. But I will tell you the 4th of July is more important to be than Cinco de Mayo or celebrating St. Patrick's Day.

I grew up in Lomita, California, which is about 30 minutes outside of Los Angeles. It's a very unique city in the fact that it's very diverse both ethnically and economically. Million dollar homes literally backed up to the projects in some areas. I've traveled through 34 of the

50 states, most of which without leaving the ground. It's by doing this that; you realize that we are different in a lot of ways. Life in Little Rock, Arkansas is much different than life in New York City. Same goes for when you compare Denver and New Orleans, Dallas and San Francisco, even Memphis and Cleveland.

We all have our own way of going about our lives. Some of us wake up and jump on a subway to get to our job, some of us wake up and walk outside to feed the chickens, some of us wake up and check the surf report and catch some waves.

We all have our own cultures and traditions that influence us. For breakfast some of us wake up and eat eggs and bacon, some of us wake up and eat chorizo burritos, some of us wake up and drink a green smoothie.

We all have our own way of speaking the same language. You know To(MAY)toe, To(MA)toe. Po(TAY)toe Po(TA)toe, soda, pop, y'all, you guys.

But when TIME magazine releases an addition after the 2016 election calling us "The Divided States of America", I had to ask myself the questions: Are we really as divided as the Main Stream Media makes us seem? Who are we? What's America's Identity?

That's the reason why I traveled around the country, that's the reason why I am writing this book. To find out and show who we really are!

The answer is: We are the greatest experiment in human history. For the first time, you take a people that don't look like each other, don't pray to the same god as each other, and leave it to them to reach an agreement to govern themselves. Nowhere in that formula should it result in success! But it has worked for more than 240 years.

Admittedly with a few errors along the way. But as a wise man once said "an error doesn't become a mistake until you refuse to correct it." And that's who we really are, we are a people of all colors, religions, and sexual orientations, fighting to not let errors become mistakes. We are a people that rose up and defeated a king and his most powerful army. We are a people that had a struggle within, but did the right thing and ended slavery. We are a people that saved the world not once but twice from evil. We are a people that on that dark September day, came together and showed the world that even though we had a big black eye, that we are stronger than ever. Why?

Because WE THE PEOPLE OF THE UNITED STATES OF AMERICA might have skin colors that are white, black, brown, yellow, or red. Our religions might be Christian, Jewish, Muslim, Hindu, or Buddhist. Some of us might like girls, guys, or both. Our occupations might be teacher, farmer, factory worker, truck driver, police officer, firefighter, entrepreneur, or stay at home moms or dads. But what it boils down to, is that we don't care what color your skin is, we don't care what god you worship, we don't care who you go to bed with, and we don't care what you do, just as long as you help us protect and defend our 3 unalienable rights to life, liberty, and the pursuit of happiness! We are a people that despite our differences show that we are similar in more ways than we can count, and we will not let the few things that we argue about, divide us. And for that reason, America will remain that city on the hill that the world will look to for inspiration and guidance!

So remember this the next time you're arguing with someone and they get you so mad that you just want to explode, or you are watching the news and they are telling you the country is going to hell. Remember this, we don't always have to see eye to eye. We are only responsible for our own actions. We are the only people that can divide us. We all bleed red. And WE ARE ALL AMERICANS! AND WE ARE ALL AMERICANS FIRST!